READY FOR
ANYTHING

READY FOR ANYTHING. Copyright © 2021 by St. Martin's Press.
All rights reserved. Printed in Malaysia. For information,
address St. Martin's Press, 120 Broadway, New York, NY 10271.

www.castlepointbooks.com
The Castle Point Books trademark is owned by Castle Point Publishing, LLC.
Castle Point books are published and distributed by St. Martin's Publishing Group.

Cover design by Hillary Caudle
Interior design by Amanda Richmond

ISBN 978-1-250-27551-6 (trade paperback)

Our books may be purchased in bulk for promotional, educational, or business use.
Please contact your local bookseller or the Macmillan Corporate and Premium Sales Department
at 1-800-221-7945, extension 5442, or by email at MacmillanSpecialMarkets@macmillan.com.

First Edition: 2021

10 9 8 7 6 5 4 3 2 1

READY FOR ANYTHING

A PLANNER FOR PREPARING YOUR HOME AND FAMILY FOR ANY EMERGENCY

CYNTHIA STRONG

CASTLE POINT BOOKS

NEW YORK

CONTENTS

SECTION II: ENVIRONMENTAL EMERGENCIES

SECTION III: PERSONAL EMERGENCIES

"The best preparation
for tomorrow is
doing your best today."

—H. JACKSON BROWN JR.

KEEP CALM AND PREP ON

Emergency preparedness is not about panic-buying solar-powered radios and pickling your own vegetables. It doesn't involve worrying all the time or building an underground bunker. It's about getting your ducks in a row so you can relax. You may not be able to stop an unexpected emergency from heading your way, but you can control how prepared you are to deal with it.

This little book makes it easy to stay a step ahead of disaster with simple tips and checklists that help you get organized. And when you're organized, you can handle whatever life throws at you. So don't let the threat of disaster overwhelm you. Just take prepping one page at a time, and you'll be ready for anything!

Essentials for Everyday Preparedness

ROUTINE PREPAREDNESS CHECKLIST

It's a good idea to consult this Routine Preparedness Checklist regularly (before natural disasters hit) to ensure that everything is at the ready, up to date, and in working order.

○ Flashlights and lanterns

○ Extra batteries

○ Battery-powered chargers

○ Smoke and carbon monoxide detectors

○ Exits (unblocked)

○ Security system

○ Generator

○ Insurance policy coverage

○ Emergency contact list (see page 16)

○ Important document file (see page 18)

○ Home inventory (see page 56)

○ Evacuation plan

- ○ Go bags (see page 14)

- ○ First-aid kits (see page 22)

- ○ Food supply

- ○ Pet licenses (in case you need to travel)

- ○ Pet carriers

- ○ IDs and passports

- ○ Maps and directions

"We should remember that good fortune often happens when opportunity meets with preparation."

—THOMAS A. EDISON

EMERGENCY HOME SUPPLIES CHECKLIST

Whether you use a bag, a bin, or a shelf in the basement, these are the items you'll want to gather up in a central location at home.

PERSONAL CARE ITEMS

○ 3 gallons of water per person

○ 3 days' worth of food per person (and pet)

○ First-aid kit (see page 22)

○ Hand sanitizer

○ Baby wipes

○ Toiletries (toothpaste, toothbrush, feminine hygiene products, etc.)

○ Sturdy shoes

○ Extra clothing

○ Blankets or sleeping bags

UTILITY ITEMS

○ Battery-powered radio

○ Flashlights

○ Extra batteries

○ Matches in a waterproof container

- ○ Multitool
- ○ Crescent wrench (to turn off utilities)
- ○ Duct tape
- ○ Garbage bags
- ○ Small towels
- ○ Disinfectant spray
- ○ N95 or surgical style masks
- ○ Permanent marker, pen, and paper
- ○ Manual can opener
- ○ Disposable plates
- ○ Disposable utensils

SAFETY ITEMS

- ○ Small fire extinguisher
- ○ Signal flare
- ○ Whistle

"Confidence comes from being prepared."

—JOHN WOODEN

GO BAG CHECKLIST

A go bag is a bag of supplies you can grab before leaving the house in an emergency. Although your go bag should be easy to carry, you'll want it to include as many of these items as possible. Leave room enough to toss in your important documents, cash, and prescription meds on your way out the door.

- ○ Emergency water filter
- ○ Collapsible water pouch*
- ○ Nonperishable food for 3 days
- ○ Utensils
- ○ Strong flashlight
- ○ Solar-powered charger and cords
- ○ Loud whistle
- ○ Lighter and/or matches in waterproof container
- ○ Hand sanitizer
- ○ Baby wipes
- ○ Multitool
- ○ Can opener
- ○ Carabiners

- ○ Paracord
- ○ Duct tape
- ○ Local map
- ○ Compass

SMALL FIRST-AID KIT
- ○ Bandages
- ○ Antiseptic
- ○ Gauze
- ○ Painkillers

SMALL TOILETRY KIT
- ○ Soap
- ○ Toothbrush
- ○ Toothpaste
- ○ Toilet paper
- ○ Rain poncho

- ○ Dust mask
- ○ Change of clothes
- ○ Vacuum-bagged blanket
- ○ Spare house/car keys

BABY SUPPLIES

- ○ Bottles
- ○ Formula
- ○ Diapers
- ○ Food

PET SUPPLIES

- ○ Leash
- ○ Collapsible bowls
- ○ Food
- ○ Recent family photo (for ID)
- ○ Writing materials (pen, paper, tape)
- ○ Portable phone charger and cord(s)

*Fill the water pouch with 1.5 gallons of water (per person) unless there are clean water sources you can access nearby.

TIP: For ease of carrying and practicality, your go bag should weigh less than 20 percent of your body weight.

"Plan for what is difficult while it is easy; do what is great while it is small."

—SUN TZU

EMERGENCY CONTACTS LIST

You can't count on being able to Google important numbers in an emergency. If you haven't already, take a few minutes to add all of your important contacts to your phone. Then sit down and make a physical list. A good emergency contact list should include only the numbers you're most likely to need in a hurry, organized in a way that makes it easy to get the information you need at a glance. The list at right includes most of the contacts you'll need. All you have to do is add the phone numbers.

"Knowledge is the key to survival, the real beauty of that is that it doesn't weigh anything."

—RAY MEARS

EMERGENCY CONTACTS LIST

Spouse	
Parent(s)	
Child(ren)	
Work	
School	
Landlord/HOA	
Friend/Neighbor	
Babysitter	
Petsitter	
Primary Care Physician	
Preferred Hospital	
Local Pharmacy	
Dentist	
Veterinarian	
Electric Company	
Gas Company	
Water Company	
Police Department	
Fire Department	
Poison Control	
Animal Control	

TIP: Keep one copy of this list on the fridge, and another in your go bag.

IMPORTANT DOCUMENTS CHECKLIST

These days, you can access a lot of information online. (Just make sure you remember your passwords.) Other important documents can be stored on your phone or in the cloud. But an inexpensive waterproof and fireproof pouch can be a portable lifesaver for hard-to-replace documents like passports and birth certificates. Here's the information you'll want to have gathered in the pouch or in a folder on your laptop:

- ○ Insurance policies (home, auto, life)
- ○ Updated home inventory
- ○ Pictures of your property
- ○ Birth certificate
- ○ Marriage certificate or divorce papers
- ○ Adoption papers
- ○ Social Security card
- ○ Passport
- ○ Driver's license

- ○ Will and advance healthcare directive
- ○ Financial assets
- ○ Real estate documents
- ○ Other asset information
- ○ Loan documents
- ○ Pictures of prescription medications
- ○ Important medical records
- ○ Pet's licensure and vaccination record

TIP: To keep everything (electronic files and paper information) in one place, consider storing files on a flash drive that you can place in the pouch.

CRITICAL SURVIVAL SKILLS CHECKLIST

Getting lost in the woods or stranded in water are extreme circumstances, but you'd be surprised by how often people unexpectedly find themselves in extreme circumstances. Learning these simple skills could prevent an illness or injury and even save your life. Luckily, they're all easy to pick up from online videos. Research each of the scenarios below and check them off when you feel you have learned enough.

○ Using a fire extinguisher

○ Starting a fire

○ Signaling for help

○ Finding and purifying water

○ Tying knots

○ Building a makeshift shelter

○ Administering first-aid

○ Administering CPR

○ Identifying edible/ poisonous plants

○ Fishing and hunting

○ Swimming

○ Escaping icy water

○ Escaping quicksand

○ Navigating

PRE-WILDFIRE EVACUATION CHECKLIST

Give your home a fighting chance by starving the fire and making sure emergency responders have what they need.

WHEN YOU HAVE SOME TIME

○ Check go bags

○ Gather important documents

○ Review evacuation plan with friends and family

○ Clear fallen branches and brush

○ Remove branches hanging over the house or lower than 15 feet from the ground

○ Clean gutters

○ Keep grass cut and watered

○ Keep fire tools handy (axes, shovels, rakes, buckets, ladders)

○ Confine pets to one room (so they're easy to evacuate)

○ Move patio furniture, lawnmowers, toys, and anything else that's flammable at least 30 feet away from the house

WHEN THINGS GET SERIOUS

○ Put go bags in the car

○ Get pets ready to go (on leash or in carriers)

○ Move farm animals to safety

- ○ Close windows and doors (leave them unlocked)
- ○ Remove flammable curtains or shades
- ○ Move furniture away from windows
- ○ Shut off air conditioning and automatic garage door openers
- ○ Turn off gas at the meter and blow out pilot lights
- ○ Turn off and move propane tanks
- ○ Turn off sprinklers (they can reduce water pressure)
- ○ Connect garden hoses to outside faucets
- ○ Leave lights on, inside and out

BONUS POINTS FOR...

- ○ Leaving buckets of water around the exterior of the house
- ○ Wetting down the roof and lawn
- ○ Sealing vents with plywood or commercial seals
- ○ Checking on your neighbors and helping them prep
- ○ Backing your packed car into your driveway so you're ready to go at a moment's notice
- ○ Keeping an eye on alerts and leaving before an emergency evacuation order

"There's no harm in hoping for the best as long as you're prepared for the worst."

—STEPHEN KING

FIRST-AID KIT CHECKLIST

A fully stocked first-aid kit is a must-have when prepping for any disaster. Try to squeeze in as many of these items as possible. For winter injuries, you may want to add heat-therapy patches.

- ○ 25 adhesive bandages (assorted sizes)
- ○ 1 roll adhesive cloth tape
- ○ 1 roll 3-inch gauze
- ○ 1 roll elastic bandage
- ○ 2 absorbent compress dressings
- ○ 5 (3x3-inch) sterile gauze pads
- ○ 5 (4x4-inch) sterile gauze pads
- ○ 5 cotton swabs
- ○ 1 tube antibiotic ointment
- ○ 1 tube hydrocortisone cream
- ○ 1 small jar petroleum jelly
- ○ 1 small bottle saline solution
- ○ 5 individually packaged antiseptic wipes
- ○ 2 packets aspirin
- ○ 2 packets preferred pain reliever
- ○ 2 packets antihistamines

- ○ Digital thermometer
- ○ 1 emergency blanket
- ○ 2 instant cold packs
- ○ 2 triangular bandages (for use as a sling or tourniquet)
- ○ 1 protective mask
- ○ 2 pairs large non-latex gloves
- ○ Scissors
- ○ Tweezers
- ○ Personal medications and auto-injector of epinephrine
- ○ Emergency first-aid guide

TIP: Buy a ready-made first-aid kit with a little room to grow, then add in whatever's missing. And check expiration dates at least once a year, adding any expired items to your next shopping list.

"Your body is your most priceless possession. Take care of it."

—JACK LALANE

AFFAIRS IN ORDER CHECKLIST

Dealing with the responsibilities of settling a loved one's affairs on top of your grief can feel impossible. Use this checklist to help you get through it, one step at a time.

- ○ Get a legal pronouncement of death

- ○ Tell friends and family

- ○ Secure any property, vehicles, and valuables

- ○ Make arrangements for pets and plants

- ○ Forward the mail

- ○ Review funeral and burial plans

- ○ Make funeral and burial (or cremation) arrangements

- ○ Request 10 certified copies of the death certificate (used to close accounts)

- ○ Locate the will and executor

- ○ Meet with an estate-planning attorney

- ○ Contact a CPA to help with taxes

- ○ Take the will to probate court

- ○ Create an inventory of assets

○ Make a list of bills to settle

○ Cancel services and memberships

○ Cancel the drivers' license

○ Notify the Social Security Administration, life insurance companies, financial institutions and advisers, and credit agencies

○ Close credit card accounts

○ Delete or memorialize social media accounts

○ Close email accounts

TIP: Consider using the information in this list to help you get your own affairs in order. Not only will you be doing your loved ones a favor (in the hopefully very distant future), you may also benefit from having your life more organized.

RECESSION CHECKLIST

Start taking these simple steps now to ensure that you're in a good place when the next recession hits.

FINANCES

○ Make your savings automatic

○ Look for painless ways to cut spending

○ Pay down high-interest debt

○ Move some savings to higher-interest CDs

○ Consider refinancing your mortgage with lower rates

○ Avoid taking on new debt

WORK

○ Assess the health of your job/company

○ Update your skillset

○ Reach out to your network

○ Start a side hustle

○ Review your investments

ROUTINE HEALTH CHART

Stave off medical and financial emergencies by keeping up with routine doctor visits and making sure everyone in your family does the same.

APPOINTMENT TYPE	PROVIDER NAME	DATE/TIME OF APPOINTMENT
Annual Checkup		
Dermatologist		
Cardiologist		
Gynecologist		
Dentist		
Eye Exam		
Mammogram		
Colonoscopy		
Bloodwork		
Pediatric Checkup(s)		

EXPENSE-CUTTING CHECKLIST

Just as the best time to look for a job is before you need one, the best time to reduce your expenses is before you're forced to. Things you can do to help in just a few minutes include:

CUT YOUR SPENDING

○ Cut cable in favor of a streaming service

○ Freeze or cancel unnecessary memberships

○ Ask for a lower or promotional rate on your credit cards

○ Shop for a cheaper cellphone plan

○ Shop for cheaper car and property insurance

CURB YOUR SPENDING

○ Use a cash-envelope system*

○ Cancel store-specific credit cards

○ Designate spend-free days to interrupt spending habits

○ Shop with a list (and stick to it)

○ Unsubscribe from all marketing emails and catalogues

FOCUS ON SAVING

○ Sign up for a free budgeting app

○ Open an emergency-specific high-interest savings account

○ Set up automatic transfers to your savings account

○ Write down everything you purchase

*In a cash-envelope system, you label each of several envelopes with a budget category (groceries, gas, etc.) and fill it with the amount of cash you've budgeted for that month. The goal is to spend only as much money as you have in the envelopes.

"One cannot be prepared for something while secretly believing it will not happen."

—NELSON MANDELA

Environmental Emergencies

HEAT WAVES

Heat waves may seem like a minor inconvenience in the age of air conditioning, but they happen to be the deadliest of all weather-related events. Overloaded circuits can lead to power outages, which makes cooling off more difficult. And many people—including children, the elderly, and those who work in hot, humid conditions—are at a higher risk for heat-related illnesses. Knowing what to watch out for could just save a life.

POWER OUTAGE PREP

Heat waves and power outages go hand in hand, thanks to air conditioners overloading the grid. When you see a heat wave in the forecast, you should:

- Add appliance thermometers to both your refrigerator and freezer.

- Have a cooler and frozen ice packs handy.

- Fill additional containers with drinkable water and freeze them.

- Move spare food items (milk, meat, leftovers) from the refrigerator to the freezer.

- Stock up on shelf-stable food (so you can keep your refrigerator closed).

- Stock up on flashlights and batteries.

FOOD SAFETY

A power outage during a heat wave can threaten your food supply. According to the Food and Drug Administration (FDA), a closed refrigerator will stay cool for 4 hours, a half-full freezer will stay cold for 24 hours, and a full freezer will stay cold for 48 hours. But if any of them hits 40 degrees Fahrenheit for more than 2 hours—or if the power is out for more than 4 hours—it's time to toss the contents. Better safe than sorry! To help keep food fresh, you can move it to coolers filled with ice when it looks like the power will be out for more than 4 hours.

Use this space to keep track of how long the power is out:

Date/time of outage: _____ / _____

Date/time of outage: _____ / _____

Date/time of outage: _____ / _____

Date/time of outage: _____ / _____

Date/time of outage: _____ / _____

Date/time of outage: _____ / _____

Date/time of outage: _____ / _____

Date/time of outage: _____ / _____

> TIP: Replace any refrigerated medication if you're without power for more than 4 hours. Also, talk to your medical provider about making a power-outage plan for any medical devices that require electricity.

TREATING
HEAT-RELATED ILLNESS

Knowing the signs of heat-related illness and how to deal with them can be the difference between life and death. If you notice that you or anyone else is suffering from these symptoms, act quickly.

Heat Cramps

Heat cramps are an early sign that the body isn't coping well with heat. People usually feel these muscle pains and cramps in their legs and abdomen.

- Move the person to a cool location, stretch them out, and gently massage the affected area.

- Have them drink something containing electrolytes, such as a sports drink, fruit juice, or milk.

TO DO

○ Know the signs of heat illness

○ Watch yourself and others for symptoms

Heat Exhaustion

You'll usually see heat exhaustion in people who work or exert themselves in a hot, humid environment, such as firefighters, athletes, and factory workers. Symptoms include headache, nausea, dizziness, weakness, and exhaustion as well as cool, moist, pale, or flushed skin.

- **Move the person to a cool, well-ventilated location.**

- **Remove as much clothing as possible and apply cool, wet towels to the skin. (A cool shower can also help.)**

- **Have them drink small amounts of a beverage containing electrolytes—about 4 ounces every 15 minutes.**

- **If things get worse or the person loses consciousness, call 9-1-1 or your local paramedics.**

Make a plan to stay cool when the heat index rises to 91°F or higher:

_____

_____

_____

_____

_____

_____

_____

_____

GIVE YOURSELF A BREAK

The heat index is what your body feels when heat and humidity are combined. When it starts to climb above 100 degrees Fahrenheit, give yourself permission to slow down and take care.

- **Skip workouts.** If you absolutely have to be outside in the sun, wear loose-fitting, lightweight clothing in light colors.

- **Relax in air-conditioning.** If you don't have air-conditioning at home, spend the day at a movie theater, library, or mall.

- **Avoid fans.** They give you a false sense of comfort but can actually make the heat worse and even lead to heat stroke.

- **Drink plenty of water.** Don't wait until you feel thirsty—at that point you're already dehydrated. If you're outside during a hot day, up your fluid intake to 4 cups of water per hour.

- **Eat salty snacks.** This may seem counterintuitive, but you need to replenish the sodium your body loses through sweat.

"Safety is something
that happens between your
ears, not something you
hold in your hands."

—JEFF COOPER

HEAT STROKE

The deadliest of the heat-related illnesses, heat stroke usually occurs when someone has ignored the symptoms of heat exhaustion. Signs include extremely high temperature; red skin; losing consciousness; confusion; weak, rapid pulse; shallow, rapid breathing; vomiting; and seizures. The person may or may not be sweating.

- Call 9-1-1 immediately.

- Move the person into a tub or shower of cold water.

- Apply towels dipped in ice water to the skin or even cover the person with bags of ice.

> **TIP:** Do not ever leave a child, elderly adult, or pet in the car on a hot day—not even when you think you'll be back soon. Even with the windows rolled down, temperatures above just 70 degrees Fahrenheit can turn a car into an oven within minutes.

"Knowledge is
the antidote to fear."

—RALPH WALDO EMERSON

EARTHQUAKES

Many people think of earthquakes as confined to the West Coast, and for good reason. It sits on the Ring of Fire, a 24,000-mile-long path along which 75 percent of earthquakes occur. But earthquakes can and do happen anywhere. When they do, they may bring with them power outages, landslides, floods, fires, avalanches, and even tsunamis. You can't know when an earthquake will strike, but you can learn how to deal with one safely.

THE RIGHT WAY TO REACT

When you feel that first tremor, do *not* move to a doorway or run outside. Instead, remember to drop, cover, and hold on.

- **Drop:** Dropping to your hands and knees prevents you from being knocked over and allows you to crawl to safety.

- **Cover:** Cover your head and neck with your arm and cover your body with a piece of furniture, such as a table or desk. If you can't get to a table, head for an interior wall (away from windows). Stay crouched down to protect your vital organs.

- **Hold On:** Hold onto the item sheltering you. If you can't find shelter, hold onto your head and neck with both arms while crouching down.

> **TIP:** If you're in a car when an earthquake strikes, pull over (preferably away from any structures), set your parking brake, and shelter in place until it stops.

TO DO

- ○ Practice earthquake protocol with family

- ○ Post "Drop, Cover, and Hold On" where all can see

EARTHQUAKE-PROOF YOUR HOME

Ensuring that heavy and breakable objects are safely tucked away or secured is always smart, but it's even more essential if you live in an earthquake-prone area. Here's a list of tasks to help minimize the danger to you, your family, and your home if an earthquake occurs.

- Secure heavy furniture

- Store breakables in latched (and secured) cabinets

- Store heavier items on the lowest shelves

- Use picture hangers instead of nails

- Move heavy objects (like mirrors) away from where you spend your time

- Keep toxic or flammable items locked away

- Secure your water heater and appliances to the wall

- Keep big, heavy furniture or objects away from doors (for easy escape)

BE PREPARED WITH LOTS OF KITS AND SUPPLIES

You never know where you'll be when an earthquake hits. And although you usually won't have the opportunity to evacuate before one, you may have to head to safety afterward. That's why it's so important to pack four sets of emergency supplies: a go bag (see page 14), a car kit, a work kit, and an Emergency Home Supplies Checklist (see page 12). Don't let that overwhelm you, though. From travel-size toiletries to bandages and pens, you probably have more than a few of these things lying around already.

Make a list of items you have lying around the house that you can add to your emergency supply kits:

_____

_____

_____

_____

_____

_____

TO DO

- ○ Check your home for spare supplies
- ○ Make a list of what you need

FIVE WAYS YOU CAN PREP FOR AN EARTHQUAKE RIGHT NOW

1. Choose a place away from your kitchen for your at-home emergency kit. That way, if the kitchen becomes inaccessible, you will still have access to emergency food and water.

2. Take a look at the Emergency Home Supplies Checklist on page 12 and the First-Aid Kit Checklist on page 22, and see which items you already have to spare.

3. Make a list of the things you need to order or shop for to fill your home kit and first-aid kit and where you can get them.

4. Add to that a list of nonperishable foods your family likes. Granola bars, crackers, cookies, and jars of peanut butter make great additions.

5. Collect all the necessary items for your kits and place them in a secure location. Let everyone in the family know they're there.

> **TIP:** If you can't secure these items today, mark a date and time in your calendar to get what you need. (We often put off what isn't scheduled.)

TURN OFF UTILITIES

Natural gas leaks and explosions following a disaster like an earthquake can contribute to a large number of fires. When you smell gas or hear a blowing or hissing sound, you should open the windows, turn off the gas, and get out of the house before calling the gas company.

> **TIP:** Cracked pipes after an earthquake can pollute your water supply, so consider turning off your water until the authorities tell you it's safe to turn it back on.

TO DO

- ○ Learn to spot the warning signs of a gas leak
- ○ Review how to shut off utilities
- ○ Share this info with all household members

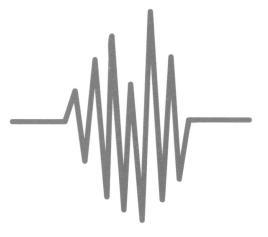

EMERGENCY SHUTOFF INSTRUCTIONS

Write down the steps for turning off each utility, then share them with everyone in your household. Consider posting instructions at each shutoff location, too.

Water (include location of main shutoff valve):

_____

_____

_____

_____

Electricity (include location of circuit breaker):

_____

_____

_____

_____

Natural gas (include location of shutoff valve):

_____

_____

_____

_____

IN THE AFTERMATH

Your first priority after a quake is personal safety. Do an injury check on yourself and your family before quickly and carefully surveying the damage. Watch for debris, broken glass, downed electrical lines, and small fires (keep that fire extinguisher handy). Because of the risk of aftershocks and secondary disasters, you should also be tuned in to local authorities by way of radio, TV, or even social media and have your go bag ready. (See page 14.)

Locate a battery-operated or solar-powered radio to use in emergencies. Make a list of information sources you can tune into if a disaster hits:

_____

_____

_____

_____

_____

_____

_____

TO DO

○ Check your go bag

○ Find your local emergency information

"We cannot stop natural disasters, but we can arm ourselves with knowledge."

—PETRA NEMCOVA

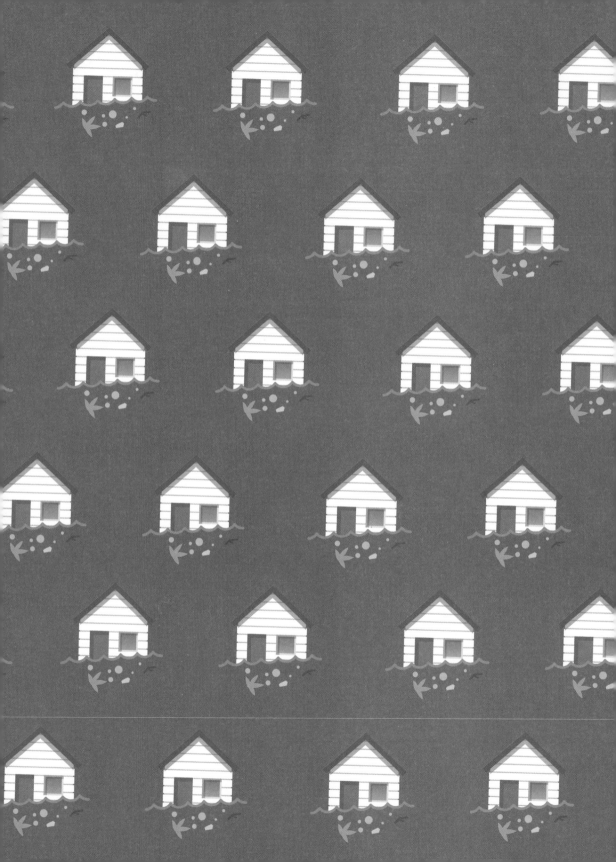

FLOODS

Hurricanes and wildfires might make the news more often, but floods are actually the most common type of natural disaster. They can be caused by torrential rain or melting snow, breaking levies and dams, rising bodies of water, storm surge, and tsunamis. And they can become a problem faster than you realize—just six inches of water is enough to knock you off your feet and make your car float. By taking a few small steps now, you can save yourself some big headaches later.

FIRST THINGS FIRST

Step one is knowing which types of flooding to prepare for. While excessive rain and snowmelt can cause flooding almost anywhere, you're more likely to experience a flood if you live in a floodplain or near bodies of water. Talk to your local emergency services providers, or check online with FEMA, to find out whether you're in a high-risk area. If so, sign up for local emergency alerts. A flood or flash warning means it's time to move to higher ground.

TIP: Flood insurance is a must if you live in a flood-prone area. Typically, you'll need to request it as an add-on to your property insurance policy.

TO DO

○ Research your home's flood risk

○ If there's moderate to high risk, research flood insurance

FLOODWATERS RISING

Water can be incredibly powerful when moving and incredibly toxic when still, making flooding one of the most destructive natural disasters you can face. Do *not* walk or drive through floodwaters, which can be deeper and more dangerous than they appear. If your car does get stuck in water, get out and move to higher ground as soon as it's safe to do so.

If you have been issued a flood warning, you should:

- Turn off utilities (if told to do so) and unplug electronics

- Wrap valuables in plastic

- Move valuables and electronics to the highest level possible

- Choose an evacuation route that avoids floodwaters

- Grab your go bags (page 14) and evacuate to higher ground

TAKE STOCK *BEFORE* A
FLOOD WREAKS HAVOC

Long before flooding becomes a possibility, make sure you have a detailed home inventory tucked away in a waterproof safe and/or stored on a cloud service with the rest of your important documents. Not only will a home inventory help you determine how much insurance coverage you need, it will also help you make quick work of claims if you experience property damage.

How to Make a Home Inventory

You'll find plenty of apps for the job, but you can also make a simple inventory by hand.

1. Grab a spare notebook.

2. Assign one page to each room of the house (including storage areas).

3. Create three columns on each page: Item, Value, and Date.

4 Going from room to room, list everything of value you see in the Item column.

5. In the Date column, write down approximately when you bought each item.

6. In the Value column, write down what it would cost to replace the item. (A quick online search will do.)

7. Add up all of the Value columns to determine how much insurance coverage you really need.

8. Take pictures of whole rooms and individual items as you go, and make sure you store them in a cloud service.

9. Computerize or take pictures of your list before storing the original in your waterproof safe.

Record your 10 most valuable items on the chart below to help you get started:

Item	Value	Date of Purchase

PLAN FOR THE
WHOLE FAMILY, PETS INCLUDED

Any disaster preparedness plan should include your furry family members. Make sure you have quick access to their food, leashes, collars, carriers, medications, and vaccination record, plus a recent picture (in case your pet runs off). Do *not* leave your pets behind assuming that they'll find higher ground—they depend on you for their safety.

Because public shelters may not take pets, you'll want to research pet-friendly motel and hotel chains both in your area and outside your evacuation zone. You can also make a plan with a neighbor or friend to retrieve your pets if you're not home when disaster strikes.

Pet Safety Plan

Pet-Friendly (Nearby) Accommodations: _____

_____

_____

Phone: _____

Address: _____

_____

Pet-Friendly (Distant) Accommodations: _____

_____

_____

Phone: _____

Address: _____

_____

Emergency Pet Evacuator: _____

_____

Phone: _____

Address: _____

_____

Plan: _____

_____

_____

_____

TIP: Get pets and farm animals accustomed to traveling in crates, cars, and trailers before disaster requires it.

PET FOOD

GO BAG 101

A go bag is a pre-packed bag full of emergency essentials that you can grab on your way out the door when disaster strikes. The best go bags offer a lot of storage but are easy to carry. Avoid large duffels, opting instead for a water-resistant hiking backpack with a chest strap. Each family member should have one that's tailored to them in both size and contents. Parents can carry the bulk of the emergency items while kids' packs can include their clothes, toiletries, and activities. Refer back to page 14 for a complete list of items to put in your go bag. If you have time, you'll want to place additional resources in your car:

- Clothing

- Sturdy shoes

- Sleeping bag(s)

- Waterproof tarp

- Toiletries (beyond the basics)

- Hygiene products

TIP: Keep in mind that you're packing not just for your destination but also in case you get waylaid en route.

CAR MAINTENANCE AND SAFETY

Putting off that routine car maintenance may not seem like a big deal. But if you need to get away in a hurry, you're going to want your car to be in tip-top shape. Stock it not only with an emergency kit and small first-aid kit but also an emergency escape tool. Luckily, these are easy to find online and in stores. If your car ends up under water, the pressure can make it all but impossible to open your door. A tap with one of these tiny tools will break your window and allow you to escape. Most also include a seatbelt cutter, which can come in handy in any accident.

Make a list of emergency items you already have in your car and ones you need to buy (and then schedule a time to shop for them):

_____

_____

_____

_____

_____

_____

_____

TO DO

- ○ Pack a car kit
- ○ Schedule regular maintenance

HURRICANES

Thanks in large part to climate change, hurricane season is getting longer, stronger, and more destructive every year. With these violent storms often comes flooding, property damage, and power outages. And even if you don't live on the coast, you could be affected by a similar weather event called a *derecho*. Make sure you're protected from the worst these storms have to offer by using the off-season and media coverage to your advantage.

YEAR-ROUND HURRICANE PREP

Disaster preparedness is a marathon, not a sprint. It's a habit you build over time. In addition to going through the Routine Preparedness Checklist on page 10, take these small steps throughout the off-season so that you're not scrambling when a hurricane hits.

- Clean out rain gutters and downspouts

- Take care of any drainage issues in your yard

- Buy or make storm shutters

- Clear out a storage space for outdoor furniture, toys, and trash cans

- Designate a windowless interior "safe room"

- Look into flood insurance

"Start where you are.
Use what you have.
Do what you can."

—ARTHUR ASHE

DAYS BEFORE A HURRICANE

More often than not, you'll have at least a little warning before the storm hits. Take this time to check that your:

- Outdoor furniture, toys, and trash cans are put away or tucked closely against the house.

- Trees are trimmed and yard is clear of any debris.

- Refrigerator is on its coldest setting.

- Phones are charged.

- Shelter-in-place supplies are ready. (See the Emergency Home Supplies Checklist on page 12.)

- Go bags are fully stocked and ready in case of evacuation.

- Gas tanks (car and home) are full.

- Pets are safely inside with everything they need.

- Safe room (or hallway or closet) is clear.

- Storm shutters are in place.

RIDING OUT A HURRICANE

Designate a place in your home where you can ride out the storm—preferably an interior room without windows. The space should be able to accommodate everyone in the house (including pets). In the days before a storm, stock that space with supplies from your Emergency Home Supplies Checklist (page 12), including food, water, flashlights, and your first-aid kit.

> **TIP:** Candles are great in a pinch, but they're also temporary and a fire hazard. And flashlights only illuminate small areas. Your best bet is to have at least one really good camping lantern in your home.

TO DO

○ Identify your hurricane "safe room"

○ Invest in a camping lantern

HEADING TO SAFETY

Most areas at high risk for hurricanes have established alert systems and evacuation plans. Take a minute right now to look into yours and make sure you're signed up for notifications. (You can do an online search, look at your county's website, or call your local emergency services.) Make some notes below based on what you find out:

_____

_____

_____

_____

_____

_____

_____

_____

_____

_____

_____

_____

> **TIP:** If you do have to evacuate, lock up. During other kinds of emergencies, you may want firefighters to have access to your house. But during hurricanes and floods, thieves will often take advantage of evacuations, especially if you're away for a few days.

KNOW ALL THE FACTS (AND MYTHS) ABOUT HURRICANE PREP

Some hurricane protocols may be more tried than true. Here are the important caveats that no one tells you:

Tape on the Windows is Not Enough

Tape on windows may stop them from shattering everywhere, but it won't stop them from breaking. For that, you'll need to install storm shutters or pre-cut, ½-inch marine plywood.

Bathtub Water is Not Drinkable

Because a power outage can cut off your water supply, you'll want to fill bathtubs and sinks with water. But this water is *not* for drinking or cooking; it can lead to lead poisoning. It's for flushing toilets, cleaning floors, and washing clothes.

Use Gas Only for Cooking

Many people with gas heat have electric blowers, rendering the heat useless during a power outage. You can still use your gas stove to cook, but never use it to heat your home. Not only is this inefficient as a heating method, it can also lead to carbon monoxide poisoning.

Store Food in Coolers, Not Outside

Storing food in coolers of ice is a great way to preserve it. But don't simply put food outside, even if it's cold. You have no way to gauge the food's temperature, and it can attract wildlife.

Make a plan for how you'll get warm (without using gas) if the power goes out during low temperatures:

_____

_____

_____

_____

_____

_____

_____

_____

_____

_____

TORNADOES

What Americans refer to as "Tornado Alley" isn't the only stretch of the U.S. that's affected by tornadoes. In fact, all fifty states encounter them, with Florida hosting the most. You may also come across other extreme weather events in your lifetime: tornado-like microbursts (powerful air shooting out of a thunderstorm), waterspouts (tornadoes occurring over water), and landspouts (half tornado, half dust storm). Even when you're lucky enough to escape a direct hit, nearby wind damage and debris from any of these events can cause power outages, road blockages, water shutoffs, and more. With a little information, you can be ready for whatever a tornado throws at you.

MAKE A PLAN FOR TORNADOES

With so little warning before a tornado, odds are good that not everyone will be home when one hits. It's important to have a plan of action for every place your family frequents.

Do these three things right now:

1. Choose a safe place to shelter at home.

2. Ask your workplace(s) and kids' school(s) about their emergency protocols.

3. Communicate the plans to the whole family.

PROTECT YOUR HOME

Preparing your home for a tornado is a lot like preparing it for a hurricane (see "Days Before a Hurricane" on page 65). Keep your yard neat and storage available for outdoor furniture and toys year-round so that you're ready whenever disaster strikes. If you live in an area prone to tornadoes, you may also want to invest in roof reinforcements and garage doors that are rated for wind pressure. Both of these things can be installed by professionals and may just save your home.

Spend five minutes walking around the outside of your home right now, and make a list of anything you need to do to prepare it for a tornado:

TO DO

○ Tidy up your yard

○ Clear out a storage space for yard items

WATCH THE WEATHER

Although tornadoes don't offer the same advance warning as hurricanes, certain weather conditions do lend themselves to tornado creation. Watching for them can give you just enough time to get to safety. Keep an eye on local news and weather stations for these terms:

- **Tornado Watch.** Conditions are ripe for a tornado. Together with your family, quickly put away any outdoor furniture and make sure you're ready to shelter with your Emergency Home Supplies Checklist (see page 12).

- **Tornado Warning**. A tornado has touched down nearby. Get everyone into your chosen shelter immediately and hunker down until you get the all-clear.

SPOT THE SIGNS

If you can't access weather information, keep an eye on the sky for these signs of an impending tornado:

- A dark green- or yellow-hued sky

- A large, dark, ominous, low-lying cloud

- Larger-than-normal hail

- A roar similar in sound to a freight train or waterfall

- A whirling, amorphous cloud of debris

- Clouds moving in a circular direction

- A fully formed funnel cloud

"Being ready before the storm strikes is sometimes the difference between life and death."

—JEFF LAST

SHELTER SMART

During an active tornado, being hit by flying debris is your biggest concern. To avoid injury, you should ideally be:

1. On the lowest floor (preferably in the basement).

2. Against an interior wall.

3. Away from windows.

4. Under heavy furniture.

5. Covered with a blanket.

6. Protecting your head and neck with your hands.

> **TIP:** If you're outside when a tornado touches down, take shelter in the nearest sturdy building or lie flat in a low area (such as a ravine) and cover your head. *Never* shelter in your car, near cars, under a bridge, or in a mobile home.

Where in your home could you shelter?

_____

_____

Where in your neighborhood could you shelter?

_____

_____

PREPARE FOR THE AFTERMATH

About half of all storm-related injuries occur after the initial disaster. With tornadoes, you'll need to worry about negotiating scattered debris, crumbling structures, downed power lines, and exposed wires. Be especially careful, and equip yourself with the following items before you venture out:

- First-aid kit (see the First-Aid Kit Checklist on page 22)

- Flashlights and batteries

- Radio tuned to news and weather alerts

- Heavy, rubber-soled shoes

- Protective clothing

- Work gloves

ANIMAL WELFARE

You may want to move your furry family members to your safe haven even before your family is ready to take shelter. Animals can sense storms before we can. As one gets closer, dogs may run and cats may hide, making it impossible to take them to safety. Just in case, all pets should be microchipped. It's a simple, inexpensive procedure performed by a veterinarian at a routine visit and it exponentially increases the odds of being reunited in the event of an escape.

PET	MICROCHIP NUMBER	ADDITIONAL INFO

TIP: Never leave livestock cooped up before a hurricane or tornado. Instead, turn them loose in large pastures on high ground with access to a strong shelter or a grouping of mature trees.

"Hope for the best,
prepare for the worst."

—PROVERB

WILDFIRES

It's easy to think that only people in fire-prone areas need to worry about wildfires. But up to 90 percent of wildfires in the United States are caused by people. And those fires are made all the more powerful and dangerous by the effects of climate change, which include high temperatures and drought. That doesn't make you helpless, though. Follow these tips to defend your home against fire and ensure your safety.

A PLAN IN PLACE

Make sure you map out routes from *all* of your regular haunts—your house, your office, the kids' school, and even the grocery store. You might know your hometown like the back of your hand, but you still need to plan out a variety of evacuation routes from each place. Fear and adrenaline can hinder your ability to make decisions.

Also, plan to meet your loved ones at a safe location rather than rushing home and driving to safety together. You don't want them wasting precious time waiting for you to arrive. Use the space below to list, think through, or map out various routes to major highways.

> **TIP:** Everyone who spends time in the house should know where the fire extinguishers are and how to use them. That includes babysitters, dog walkers, and plant waterers.

_____

_____

_____

_____

_____

_____

_____

_____

_____

TO DO

○ **Stock up on fire extinguishers**

○ **Tell family members where to find them**

STAY IN THE KNOW

Wildfires are all the more dangerous because they're unpredictable, which is why it's so important to stay informed. Keep a TV or radio tuned to your local news or NOAA stations, and check your city's website regularly. Don't forget that you have a ton of information at your fingertips— literally! Follow local and regional government accounts on social media and download these helpful apps:

- The Red Cross's First Aid and Emergency apps

- Accuweather or The Weather Channel

- Google Maps

- Gasbuddy (to help you find fuel when it's scarce)

- Zello (a walkie-talkie app with emergency frequencies)

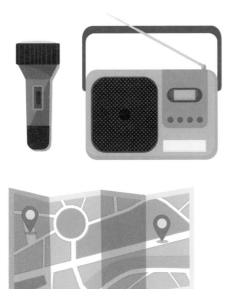

TO DO

○ Sign up for emergency safety alerts

○ Research and download new safety apps

ENSURE YOUR HEALTH

When poor air quality keeps you indoors, make sure you keep your indoor air clear (so, no candles, fires, or cooking with gas). Consider investing in a high-quality air purifier, too. And don't forget to plan for time spent inside. Fill your prescriptions ahead of time, stock two weeks' worth of groceries, and think of indoor activities to avoid going stir-crazy.

It's also very important to keep your prescriptions in stock in case of emergency. Use the chart on the page at right to track which medicines you have and which ones your family needs to restock.

TO DO

- ○ Check indoor air quality
- ○ Purchase air purifiers, replace air filters
- ○ Stock up on groceries
- ○ Stock up on medicines

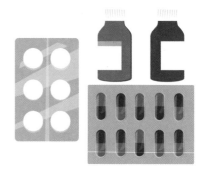

Family Medicines

Family member	Prescription name	Expiration date	Date to request refill (3-4 weeks before expiration date)

START HERE

Start to formulate your wildfire emergency plan right here and now by filling in these blanks.

FAMILY MEMBER   **CONTACT INFO**

_____ _____

_____ _____

_____ _____

_____ _____

_____ _____

_____ _____

_____ _____

_____ _____

_____ _____

EVACUATION SPOT

_____

_____

_____

EVACUATION ROUTE FROM HOME

_____

_____

_____

ALTERNATE EVACUATION ROUTE FROM HOME

_____

_____

EVACUATION ROUTE FROM (WORK/SCHOOL/OTHER)

_____

_____

MEETING PLACE IF SEPARATED

_____

_____

LOCATION OF GO BAGS

_____

_____

LOCATION OF IMPORTANT DOCUMENTS

_____

_____

OTHER IMPORTANT INFO

_____

_____

"Purpose without preparation
is meaningless."

—ANDRENA SAWYER

WINTER STORMS

You can probably ride out most winter storms with a warm cup of cocoa, a blanket, and a good book. But what happens when the heat goes out? Or the pipes burst? Or you're stuck in your car? Snow, ice, freezing rain, high wind, and extreme cold can take their toll. If you're ready for anything a winter storm can throw at you, you can turn a major problem into a minor inconvenience.

BEFORE THE STORM

Get your home ready for winter before the first snowflake falls. Additional insulation, caulking, and weather stripping can help your home retain heat during extreme cold. But once you've sealed your home against the elements, you'll need to regularly check that your carbon monoxide detectors are in working order.

TIP: Buy a generator in the spring or summer, before it becomes a hot commodity. When you use it, keep it outside and away from windows to avoid carbon monoxide poisoning.

TO DO

- ○ **Weatherize windows and doors**
- ○ **Check CO detectors**
- ○ **Research generators**

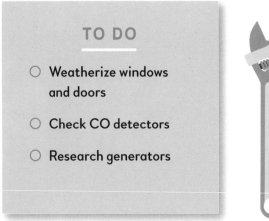

"It's better to look
ahead and prepare than
to look back and regret."

—JACQUELINE JOYNER KERSEE

WHEN THE STORM HITS

The best thing to do during a winter storm is hunker down and avoid putting yourself at risk. If you can, avoid:

- **Traveling.** Between black ice and blinding snow drifts, driving can quickly become dangerous.

- **Overexertion.** Shoveling heavy snow can do more than injure your back; it can also lead to a heart attack.

- **Exposure** to the elements. A short time in the cold can lead to frostbite and hypothermia.

Make a list of everything you'll need if you have to stay put for at least three days (and make sure you have everything before the next storm hits):

_____

_____

_____

_____

_____

_____

_____

_____

_____

_____

_____

PROTECT YOUR PIPES

When the temperature lowers, you're at greater risk of frozen pipes. Take these early precautions to keep your pipes from freezing:

- Close the garage door to protect any pipes inside.

- Open cabinets to allow heat to circulate around the plumbing. (If you have little ones, remove any harmful items from the open cabinets.)

- Let cold water drip from faucets served by outside pipes.

- Keep the thermostat set at the same temperature all day and night.

> **TIP:** In an emergency situation, prepare to have about 3 gallons of water per person per day. When storing water, avoid glass containers, which are heavy and breakable. Gallon plastic jugs of water are light, cheap, and readily accessible.

CAUGHT IN THE CAR

An unexpected storm can leave you stranded or even run you off the road. When the weather gets cold, check that your tires have plenty of tread and are filled to the right pressure. Your car should also be gassed up and fully stocked with all of these essentials to keep you warm and dry while you wait for help.

Keep tabs on your tire pressure here:

Vehicle: _____

Ideal tire pressure: _____

Last tire pressure check: _____

Vehicle: _____

Ideal tire pressure: _____

Last tire pressure check: _____

Vehicle: _____

Ideal tire pressure: _____

Last tire pressure check: _____

Vehicle: _____

Ideal tire pressure: _____

Last tire pressure check: _____

EXPOSURE TO THE ELEMENTS

I f you have to venture outside during winter weather, keep it brief and be mindful of signs of frostbite and hypothermia.

Frostbite

Signs of frostbite include numbness in the face, fingers, or toes as well as white or grayish-yellow skin and firm or waxy skin. Get into a warm room and soak the affected area in warm water. Do *not* rub the skin or use a heating pad.

Hypothermia

Signs of hypothermia include shivering, confusion, slurred speech, fumbling, drowsiness, and exhaustion. Get inside, take off any wet clothes, wrap up in blankets, and focus on warming up from the center of the body out.

Schedule a time to buy these items and add them to your car's emergency kit:

- ○ Jumper cables
- ○ Hazard triangles
- ○ Ice scraper
- ○ Traction mats
- ○ Pet-safe ice melt

- ○ Cat litter or sand (for traction)
- ○ Blankets
- ○ Hand warmers
- ○ Non-perishable snacks

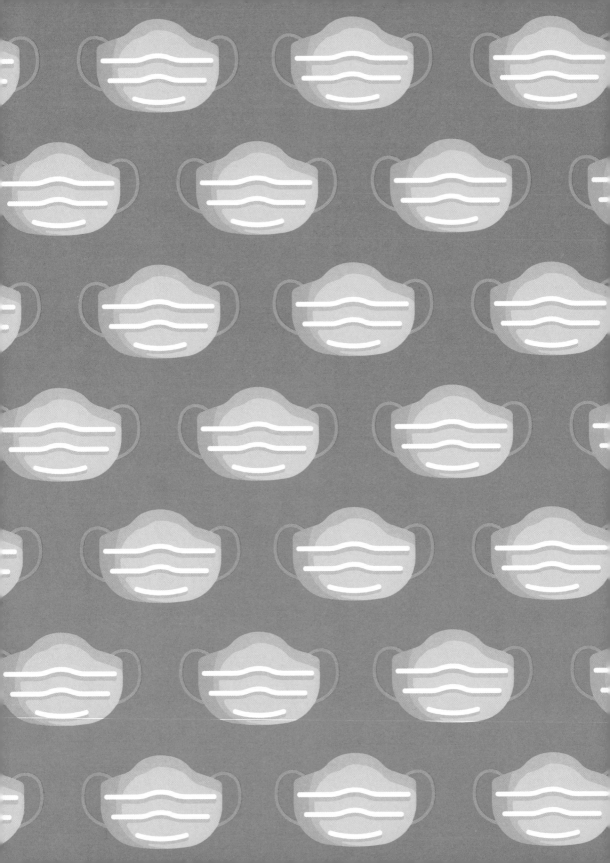

PANDEMICS

Pandemics are nothing new. From the plague to smallpox, HIV to H1N1, illnesses and viruses have always spread like wildfire through the world population. And as we become more interconnected, they spread even more easily. But COVID-19 may have been the first to bring the world's population together against a common threat. We learned first-hand that life as we all know it can change overnight. We also learned that being prepared is better than being scared.

RELY ON EXPERTS

The most important thing you can do in any health emergency is listen to the experts. During a pandemic, you'll want to rely heavily on the Centers for Disease Control (CDC) and the World Health Organization (WHO). These organizations are full of people who have devoted their lives to understanding human health and the devastating effects of pandemics. Their only goal is to protect the public.

Don't be discouraged when expert advice changes. That's how science works. Experts search meticulously for better information, and when they get it, their theories evolve and they act accordingly.

> **TIP:** Question everything that comes from well-meaning friends, social media posts, and media personalities. Always look for data to back up opinions.

"Research means that
you don't know, but
are willing to find out."

—CHARLES F. KETTERING

STOCK UP

The last thing you want to do is panic-shop in crowded stores during a pandemic. Whether you're preparing for natural disasters, personal emergencies, or medical crises, having a fully stocked home kit will keep you from frantically clearing box-store shelves. If you knew that the country would be on lockdown for one month, what items would you need to buy immediately?

> **TIP:** Using the Emergency Home Supplies Checklist on page 12 and the First-Aid Kit Checklist on page 22 as your guides, stock up year-round. For pandemic prep, add cleaning products and cold-and-flu supplies.

STAY HOME

During any pandemic, you'll naturally be more cautious about venturing out. Here are some ways you can stay safe:

- Utilize the drive-thru option at pharmacies and eateries

- Ask your health insurer to approve a 90-day supply of your medications

- Have prescriptions delivered to your home

- Subscribe to a meal delivery kit

- Order produce from a local grower who delivers

- Order online and choose the drive-up option at major stores and supermarkets

- Batch-cook and freeze meals as you get fresh ingredients (supply-chain issues may limit what you can find at the store)

"Before anything else, preparation is the key to success."

— ALEXANDER GRAHAM BELL

MAKE A QUARANTINE PLAN

As hard as you try to avoid it, you or someone else in your household may get sick. Answer these questions so you have a plan in place.

Where will the person quarantine? (Preferably with their own bathroom.)

_____

_____

_____

_____

Who will care for them?

_____

_____

_____

_____

How will you protect each other?

_____

_____

_____

_____

Who will care for others in the house, including children and pets?

_____

_____

_____

_____

PRIORITIZE SELF-CARE

Taking care of yourself means finding ways to wind down as well as pandemic-friendly ways to work out. You want your body to be able to fend off illness, so this is the time to start cementing some healthy habits. Shore up your immune system with good food, exercise, and lots of sleep. And maintain a healthy sense of optimism. With every day, we get better at understanding and dealing with these major health crises.

Make a list of the habits you'd like to improve and what you can do to improve them:

_____

_____

_____

_____

_____

_____

_____

TO DO

○ Plan healthy meals

○ Schedule regular exercise

○ Make mental health a priority

PRACTICE GOOD HYGIENE

In some countries, it's customary to wear a mask if you think you might be sick. This kind of self-awareness and health consciousness can keep whole communities safe. Here are some easy hygiene practices you can adopt to ward off illness both for yourself and your community.

- Regularly wash your hands for at least 20 seconds

- Use hand sanitizer with at least 60 percent alcohol

- Stop touching your face (especially mucous membranes)

- Keep your distance from others

- Stay home when sick

- Wear a mask if you might be contagious

- Cough or sneeze into a tissue or elbow

- Clean and disinfect surfaces regularly

- Sanitize and bandage any cuts or scrapes

TIP: Pandemics can also take a financial toll. Focus on building up your emergency savings now in case you can't work later.

"If everyone is moving forward together, then success takes care of itself."

—HENRY FORD

Personal Emergencies

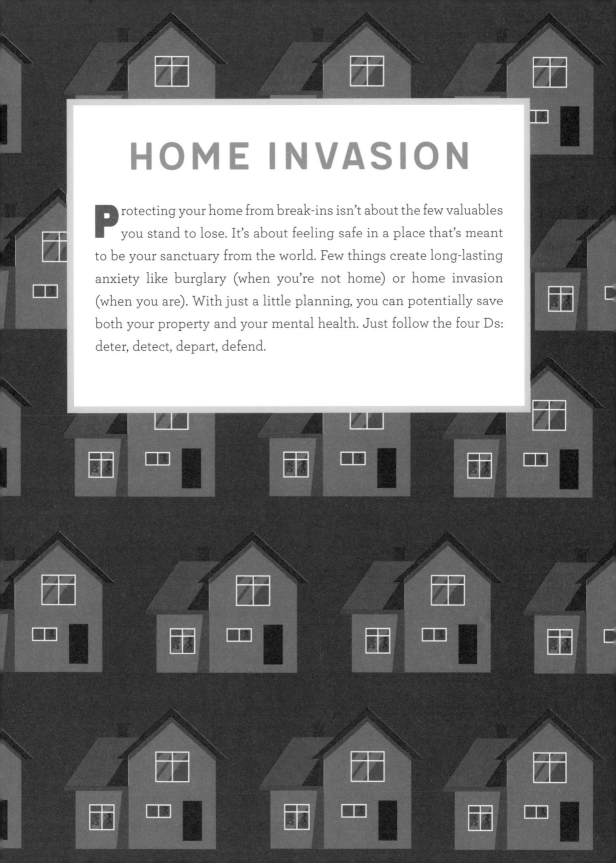

HOME INVASION

Protecting your home from break-ins isn't about the few valuables you stand to lose. It's about feeling safe in a place that's meant to be your sanctuary from the world. Few things create long-lasting anxiety like burglary (when you're not home) or home invasion (when you are). With just a little planning, you can potentially save both your property and your mental health. Just follow the four Ds: deter, detect, depart, defend.

DETER

The best protection against any intrusion is to deter it in the first place. If you can, invest in a complete security system. Here are a few other things you can do:

- **Use light.** Use smart switches or mechanical timers to turn the lights (and the TV) on when no one's home. Install motion-detector lights at multiple points outside, too.

- **Switch things up.** A predictable daily schedule can embolden would-be thieves. Make sure your routine isn't entirely predictable.

- **Make note of strangers.** Burglars often case a house before robbing it, so make note of anyone who seems to be eyeing your home. A stranger may even knock on your door to gauge whether someone's home before entering.

- **Use cameras.** Visible cameras are a great deterrent, and they're cheaper and easier to buy than ever.

DETECT

If you can't deter an intruder, you need to know the minute they break in so you can escape or hide and call 9-1-1. An inexpensive solution is to buy cameras that push alerts to your mobile phone. (You can change the settings to be more or less sensitive so your camera isn't catching shadows on the wall.) Just don't skimp on picture clarity—the footage could help police identify the intruder.

> **TIP:** Some of the smart devices you already use at home, such as Amazon Echo devices, have security capabilities, sending push notifications to your phone when the device hears glass breaking or a smoke alarm going off. Check to see what safeguards you already have.

"Forewarned is forearmed;
To be prepared is half the victory."

—MIGUEL DE CERVANTES

DEPART

If you're home during a break-in, your safety and your family's safety are your top priority. You need to keep the intruder from getting to you.

Before a Home Invasion

- Plan several escape routes

- Designate a safe spot to meet up (such as a neighbor's house)

- Make sure everyone knows the plans

- Keep your car keys near you (for both the alarm and easy escape)

- Teach kids never to answer the door alone

During a Home Invasion

- Get out of the house

- Call 9-1-1 when it's safe to do so

DEFEND

If you think you hear someone creeping around your house at night, do **not** go looking for them. Escape is your first line of defense. When that's not possible, grab whatever weapon you have at hand (a baseball bat or even a frying pan works), barricade your door, and call 9-1-1. Remember that things can be replaced. You and your family cannot.

> **TIP**: Whether you see someone lurking in your neighborhood or hear someone in your home, never hesitate to call the police. They may already be searching for the suspected prowler and need that call.

Go through your home and make a list of items you can use to barricade your door or defend yourself:

_____

_____

_____

_____

_____

_____

_____

_____

_____

THINK LIKE A THIEF

Thieves can spot a hide-a-key a mile away, and they know they'll find valuables in a locked drawer or safe. Use these five tricks to make their lives more difficult.

- **Find unique hiding places.** A quick search of "where to hide valuables" will give you all sorts of ideas, but the closet or freezer shouldn't be on your list.

- **Stay off social media.** Don't announce your vacation to anyone, let alone to the entire Internet.

- **Move the trash cans.** Look for things a thief can use to hoist themselves up to an unlocked window.

- **Use a decoy.** A cheap jewelry box full of costume jewelry and a few loose bills might keep thieves from looking any further.

- **Keep the doorway clear.** Leaving car keys just inside the door is a quick way to lose a car. Hang them far from the front door, or set them somewhere less visible to potential intruders.

BONUS: Lock your garage or shed. Thieves can use the tools they find inside to break into the house. Also, replace the short screws in your door frame with 3-inch wood screws.

TO DO

- ○ Remove climbable items under exterior windows

- ○ Reinforce door frame with longer screws

"Make preparations
in advance. You never
have trouble if you
are prepared for it."

—THEODORE ROOSEVELT

NEIGHBORHOOD WATCH

Having a good relationship with a few of your neighbors can make all the difference in protecting your home. Take a minute right now to choose a neighbor you trust. Talk to them about:

- Trading spare keys instead of hiding them

- Questioning strangers lurking around each others' homes

- Using each others' homes as your designated safe space in the event of a home invasion.

A Call Away

Record the names of your neighbors and add their contact info below. Use this as a resource in case of emergencies:

_____

_____

_____

_____

_____

_____

_____

_____

_____

_____

_____

DEALING WITH THE FALLOUT

A burglary or home invasion can be unsettling. Take these steps to deal with the physical and mental ramifications.

1. Take a little time to process what has happened.

2. Document any damage or missing items for the police through photos and notes.

3. Call your insurance company to start a claim.

4. Shore up your home security using the steps in this section.

5. Talk about the trauma with family, friends, or a licensed counselor.

> **TIP:** Having a detailed home inventory can help you deal with insurance claims. Carve out some time right now to create one using the instructions on page 56.

Make a list of ways your can make your home less vulnerable to intruders:

_____

_____

_____

_____

_____

_____

_____

_____

ILLNESS OR INJURY

Your inbox is overflowing, your to-do list is out of control, and you don't have time to get sick or injured. But if you don't want a major health issue to knock you off your feet, you need to make the time to plan for and, hopefully, prevent it. Some health problems are unpredictable. But most we see coming and still don't bother to course-correct. Start forming these good habits today and you could save yourself a world of hurt tomorrow.

TAKE CARE OF YOURSELF

Do you realize how much pain and expense you can prevent with some simple self-care? Maintaining a healthy weight, for example, can help you avoid costly medical issues such as diabetes, and surgeries with painful recoveries, such as knee replacement. As much as you can, make sure you:

- Eat nutritious foods.

- Watch your weight.

- Stretch and move your body.

- Get routine vaccinations.

- Tend to your mental health.

- Schedule annual checkups. (Don't forget your specialists!)

TO DO

○ Schedule annual check-up

○ Add one healthy habit to my daily schedule

ASK FOR HELP

Most people hate asking for help. But when you're not feeling well or you're recovering from an injury, you can't afford to be stubborn. You could make things worse and extend your recovery time. The quickest way to get back on your feet is to let others lend you a hand. List some people below who you would feel comfortable reaching out to in times of illness or injury:

_____

_____

_____

_____

_____

_____

_____

"An ounce of prevention
is worth a pound of cure."

— BENJAMIN FRANKLIN

CHECK YOUR BENEFITS

In addition to disability insurance, many workplaces offer wellness incentives. (If you don't have disability insurance through work, it may be worth buying on your own.) Ask your human resources department whether they offer the following benefits. Some may even offer money or rewards for healthy choices.

- Fitness class reimbursement

- Health coaching

- Mental health resources

- Free membership to health apps

- Free weight-loss coaching

- Help to quit smoking

TIP: More than 4 million workers suffer a serious job-related illness or injury each year. Get proactive to make sure you're not one of them. Insist on being given the right training and equipment for your job, from ergonomic workstations to protective equipment.

"Safety is not
a gadget but a
state of mind."

—ELEANOR EVERET

DON'T PROCRASTINATE

You never know what's going to happen tomorrow. But if you get sick or injured, you're going to wish you had checked off the most important things on your to-do list. Make a list of all the things—small and large—that you would do if you knew you'd be out of commission for two weeks. That can be anything from laundry and meal prep to finishing your work ahead of deadline.

Your Top 10 To-Dos

Rank your to-do list items in order of importance and start crossing them off, from top to bottom.

1. _____
2. _____
3. _____
4. _____
5. _____
6. _____
7. _____
8. _____
9. _____
10. _____

Learn First-Aid Now

You should always have a fully stocked first-aid kit in your home and a smaller version in your car. (Use the First-Aid Kit Checklist on page 22 as a guide to creating yours.) But tools are only as good as the person using them. Learning basic first-aid—like how to wrap a sprained ankle—*before* you need it is a much better plan than trying to read a manual when you or your loved ones are in pain.

TO DO

○ Add first-aid kit to car and home

○ Sign up for first-aid class

"An hour of planning can save you ten hours of doing."

—DALE CARNEGIE

DEATH

Even when death is imminent and inevitable, you can never prepare for the mental and emotional toll it takes. What you can prepare for is the brain fog that will set in at the same time as you're expected to make a thousand decisions and arrangements. Keeping tidy records, discussing final wishes, and preparing for final arrangements now can save you and your loved ones from additional and unnecessary stress during an already difficult time.

AFFAIRS IN ORDER

None of us knows how much time we have, and none of us wants to leave a mess for their loved ones to decode. Using the Important Documents Checklist on page 18 as a guide, gather all of your important documents in one secure place and encourage loved ones to do the same. Getting organized now will give you both peace of mind so you won't struggle unnecessarily whenever that time comes.

TO DO

○ Gather important documents

○ Include any necessary passwords

"Preparing for death is one of the most empowering things you can do. Thinking about death clarifies your life."

—CANDY CHANG

SECURING A DIGITAL FOOTPRINT

Between email, social media, membership sites, streaming services, and online accounts, we all have considerable digital footprints. You'll need a complete accounting of these sites, including usernames and passwords, to close them and settle an estate. Help loved ones (spouses, parents, etc.) create a chart like the one below, and encourage them to keep it updated and stored in a safe place you can both access.

TYPE	WEBSITE	USERNAME	PASSWORD
Email account			
Social media account			
Checking account			
Savings account			
Credit card account			
Retirement account			
Insurance provider (car)			
Insurance provider (life)			
Insurance provider (home)			
Membership site			
Streaming service			

TALK TO A LAWYER

As easy as it is to draw up documents using online software, you'll still want to consult a lawyer for any end-of-life arrangements. Laws vary from state to state, and a small mistake could easily result in big problems, such as a will being invalidated. Plus, having a third party handle some of the details means less worry for you and your loved ones.

> **TIP:** There are planners you can buy dedicated to helping you organize someone's affairs (including your own). You can use one to determine what you need before talking to a lawyer or even have your loved ones fill one out and slip it in with their important documents to make things easy on their executor later.

TO DO

- ○ Hire an estate lawyer and a CPA
- ○ Reach out to friends and family
- ○ Delegate the tasks in the Affairs in Order Checklist on page 24

TALK TO THE PEOPLE
WHOSE JOB IT IS TO HELP

Settling someone's affairs is not a one-person job. Your loved one should have named a power of attorney (the person who makes decisions for you if you're incapacitated) and an executor (the person who carries out your decisions upon your death). If you've been named as either, you'll still need the help of professionals, such as lawyers and CPAs, as well as the support of friends and family. Delegating tasks and leaning on others is the best way to get through everything that needs to be done.

Make a list of people who can help you deal with your loss, physically or emotionally:

_____

_____

_____

_____

_____

_____

_____

_____

_____

_____

_____

_____

HONORING FINAL WISHES

Knowing what your loved ones want can be a huge relief after their passing. The best way to learn their wishes, from their medical care to their final resting place, is simply to ask them. Some people may even prefer to make arrangements in advance and save friends and family the trouble and expense. When talking to them, consider these decisions:

Do you want extraordinary measures taken, such as resuscitation and life support?

_____

_____

_____

_____

_____

_____

Do you want a funeral or wake? What should it look like? (Flowers? Music? Attire?)

_____

_____

_____

_____

_____

_____

_____

Do you want to be buried or cremated? What kind of container would you like?

_____

_____

_____

_____

_____

_____

_____

Where would you like your final resting place to be?

_____

_____

_____

_____

_____

_____

_____

_____

"All things are ready,
if our mind be so."

—WILLIAM SHAKESPEARE

MAJOR EXPENSES

Life is full of major expenses, many of them unexpected. Maybe your car breaks down or you need emergency surgery. You might have to fly out to take care of a sick family member or fork out thousands of dollars when your dog gets into some holiday treats. Obviously, your best course of action is keeping a rarely touched rainy-day fund. But when that's not possible, you still have plenty of options.

EXPECT THE UNEXPECTED

You may not know when or why you're going to get hit with a large bill, but it's bound to happen. With a little planning, you can prepare for it. You may even be able to prevent it.

Maintain Your Emergency Fund

Set up automatic deposits from your paychecks to a dedicated savings account. Even a tiny amount of money saved each week can add up quickly and save you from panicking when your water heater breaks. But remember that an emergency fund is just that. Avoid the temptation to dip into it for Christmas gifts, vacations, and routine bills.

Maintain Your Stuff

Many major expenses revolve around repairs to your property. Skip too many oil changes and you'll end up needing expensive engine repairs. Ignore a small leak and it can become major water damage. In short, a little basic maintenance can save you lots of money in the long run.

TO DO

- ○ Set up automatic deposits to savings

- ○ Get small home issues repaired to avoid big home issues

- ○ Get car tuned up

Maintain Your Health

Staying a step ahead of expensive health problems means both taking care of yourself and going in for routine checkups. Think of it this way: emergency-room co-insurance costs a lot more than your family doctor's co-pay. And early detection could save you a lot more than money; it could save your life.

Make a list of routine visits your insurance covers and the co-pays for each. Refer to the Routine Health Chart on page 27 to schedule necessary appointments.

_____

_____

_____

_____

_____

_____

_____

_____

_____

_____

_____

_____

_____

_____

_____

_____

WEDDINGS AND FAMILY EVENTS

Unexpected expenses aren't always ominous. They can also be celebratory, like when your best friend is getting married three states away. Occasions like that might cost you more money than you'd like, but not attending may come with an emotional cost. Try these tips to mitigate the expense:

- Start saving the second you receive the invitation

- Build a couple of events into your annual budget

- Be one of the first to buy off the registry

- Rent your suit or dress

- Buy a staple outfit you can dress up multiple ways

- Choose travel by car or train instead of by plane

- Split a hotel room with a friend

- Skip the hotel and look for alternative rental options

- Share rides around town

- Be picky about which events you attend

NEGOTIATE THE TOUGH STUFF

You'd be surprised at what you can negotiate, from the actual cost of services provided to interest-free payment plans. It never hurts to ask. You can even negotiate down some medical expenses. Talk to the billing department about reducing your bill or working out a payment plan. Many hospitals have charity funds for those who can't afford their treatment. What current expenses do you have that you could negotiate? List them here:

_____

_____

_____

_____

_____

_____

_____

_____

_____

_____

_____

_____

_____

_____

_____

_____

_____

INVEST IN PET INSURANCE

Owning pets is a major expense in and of itself, but emergency vet bills can reach into the thousands in a single day. And too many pet owners are forced to decide between going into debt or putting their beloved pet down, even when the illness is treatable. Avoid that heart-wrenching choice by investing in pet insurance early in your animals' lives. The younger your pet is when you get the insurance, the cheaper it'll be and the more it'll cover. And you can choose from various levels of coverage to fit your budget.

> **TIP:** Avoid costly vet bills by doing a little research on items that could harm your pets and keeping them out of reach. You'd be amazed at the everyday dangers they face, from grapes and lilies to raw bones and hair ties.

TO DO

- ○ Research pet insurance or create a pet emergency account
- ○ Clear the house of any pet hazards
- ○ Schedule routine vet visits

"Planning is bringing the future into the present so you can do something about it now."

—ALAN LAKEIN

GET A SECOND JOB

When you need money and have some spare time, a side hustle can be a viable option.

PART-TIME JOBS

- Cashier at a local store
- Babysitter, house sitter, or pet-sitter/dog walker
- Food delivery person
- Carshare driver
- Personal shopper
- Handyman
- Freelance writer/artist/designer

ONLINE SELLING

- Furniture
- Electronics
- Clothing
- Shoes
- Handbags
- Collectibles
- Books
- Handmade items

TIP: Keep the tags, manuals, and packaging of the pricier items you buy to increase their resale value later.

"Do what
you have to
do until you can do
what you want to do."

—OPRAH WINFREY

IF YOU'RE DESPERATE

When all else fails, there are a few more things you can do to find the money you need. But these should be treated as a last resort. Each comes with downsides, such as interest fees and penalties.

- Get a home-equity line of credit or loan

- Borrow against your life insurance policy

- Tap into your retirement savings

- Work with a debt consolidator

- Ask friends or family for a loan

- Downsize your home

- Sell your car in favor of public transportation

- Declare bankruptcy

Make a plan below detailing some of the steps you could take if you had to cover a large, unexpected expense.

_____

_____

_____

_____

_____

_____

_____

_____

_____

_____

_____

_____

_____

_____

_____

_____

_____

_____

_____

_____

_____

_____

_____

_____

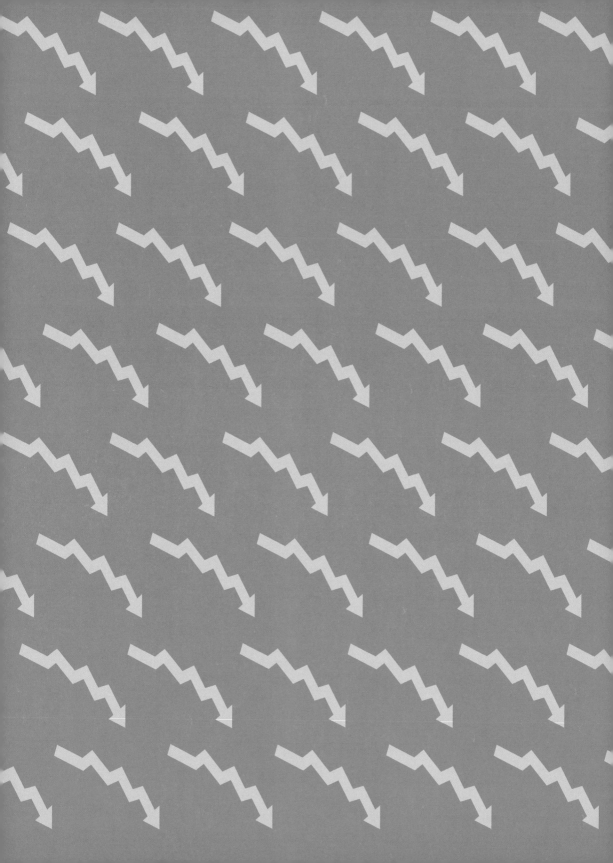

RECESSION

Recessions are common fluctuations in the market. In fact, we've had twelve of them since 1945, most of which lasted less than a year. When one hits, just remember: this too shall pass. The economy has always bounced back, and it will bounce back again. And with a few adjustments, you can ride out any bumps in the road until it does.

FOCUS ON YOUR FINANCES

You want your finances to be in the best shape possible before a recession throws a whole bunch of unpredictability into the mix. That means doing two things:

- **Build up your emergency fund.** Ideally, 20 percent of your income should go into a dedicated savings account with a competitive interest rate. When a recession seems to be looming, cut back on unnecessary spending and put that money toward your savings. Because interest rates dip during a recession, look into opening a CD account, which locks in better rates.

- **Pay down debt.** Focus on paying down your high-interest debt first. If you're not able to pay your credit card in full within a couple months, you could also look for a balance transfer offer. These allow you to transfer the debt to another card with zero interest for a year or more in exchange for a small fee (usually 3 percent of the debt).

LEAVE STOCKS ALONE

When word of a recession spreads, people tend to panic and sell their stocks. But building wealth through the stock market is a long game, and you can only win if you play. Talk to your stockbroker about shoring up your portfolio. Your stocks will bounce back when the economy does, and you'll be glad you didn't lose out on extra money.

> **TIP:** For as long as you can afford to, maintain financial momentum by continuing to pay down your debt and contribute to your retirement accounts.

"The way to cope with the future is to create it."

—ILYA PRIGOGINE

INVEST IN YOU

Layoffs are a hard reality during a recession, but versatility can be your life raft. Rather than trying to become indispensable to one particular company (which may or may not survive), focus on building out your skillset. Brainstorm all the roles and industries that might already be open to you. Add any that could be open to you if you expanded your skill set.

Skill-Building 101

Do a quick search right now and write down all the skills that you're interested in and that are in demand. Then look to see where you can learn them for free online. The more skills you acquire, the easier it will be to transition to a new position.

IN-DEMAND SKILL	ONLINE TUTORIAL

TIP: Follow the steps outlined in "Keep Your Options Open" on page 156. These job-searching strategies can help you prepare for any kind of career commotion.

REINVENT YOURSELF

Recessions have a way of restructuring the economy, giving rise to new industries and, unfortunately, debilitating some old ones. If your chosen field looks like it's about to be shaken up, take a few minutes to dream up alternative career paths. Start by listing skills that may be transferrable to a different role or a new industry.

TRANSFERRABLE SKILL	POSSIBLE USES

START A SIDE BUSINESS

Recessions are also a great opportunity to explore new ways of making money and diversifying your income. Can you monetize one of your passion projects? Having more than one income stream makes you more resilient in any kind of career or economic upset. Start small. If you do lose your job, you can use some of your time to grow your side hustle into something that may pay the bills on its own. Take a minute right now to think of five business you could start.

1. _____

2. _____

3. _____

4. _____

5. _____

"Dreaming, after all,
is a form of planning."

—GLORIA STEINEM

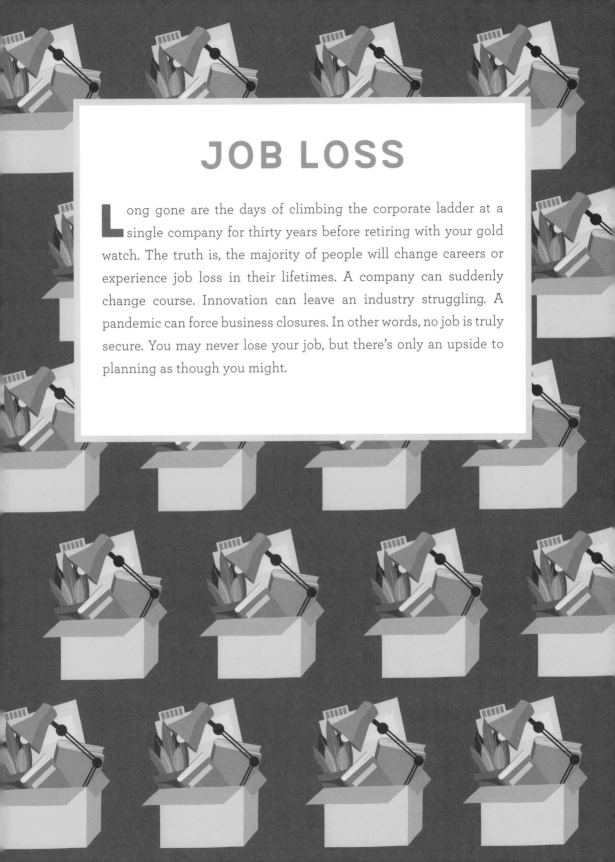

JOB LOSS

Long gone are the days of climbing the corporate ladder at a single company for thirty years before retiring with your gold watch. The truth is, the majority of people will change careers or experience job loss in their lifetimes. A company can suddenly change course. Innovation can leave an industry struggling. A pandemic can force business closures. In other words, no job is truly secure. You may never lose your job, but there's only an upside to planning as though you might.

KEEP YOUR OPTIONS OPEN

The average person will hold twelve to fifteen jobs in their lifetime—that's reason enough to keep your options open at all times. Here are five things you can do right now (and should continue to do regularly):

- Send a quick hello to someone in your network.

- Join a professional network or two.

- Write down everything you've accomplished in your career.

- Use those accomplishments to update your resume.

- Sign up for alerts from job boards like Indeed or ZipRecruiter.

> **TIP:** Keeping an ongoing file or list of accomplishments is easier than trying to think of them when you need to beef up a cover letter. You can use them to update your resume, but you can also use them to support a request for a raise or promotion.

> **TIP:** Severance is often negotiable, so don't just accept whatever you're given. Have an attorney or friend review any severance agreement before signing it.

"Prepare and prevent,
don't repair and repent."

—UNKNOWN

REACH OUT

Losing your job can make you feel isolated and embarrassed. But remember that millions of people have been there, and you have systems in place waiting to support you.

- **Your network.** Reaching out to your network is the quickest way to find work. You can avoid any awkwardness by keeping up with your work contacts regularly before you need them.

- **The government.** If you've been laid off, don't think twice before filing for unemployment. That is your money that you've been paying into the system since Day 1 on your first job. You may also find that the national Healthcare Marketplace (HealthCare.gov) is cheaper than COBRA insurance. Be honest about your income when you apply so that you're eligible for the maximum subsidy.

- **Friends and family.** Losing a job can be traumatic. Let loved ones know what you're going through so they can help. You never know— they could also be your connection to a new position.

- **Job search groups.** You'll find plenty of career coaching groups on Facebook full of people going through the same struggles. This can be a great outlet if you feel uncomfortable talking to friends and family.

TO DO

○ Email or text an old coworker to keep in touch

○ Research career coaches and resume consultants

"Do not save what
is left after spending,
but spend what is
left after saving."

—WARREN BUFFETT

CONCLUSION

Emergencies happen, but now you know how to deal with them head on. You're prepared for a power outage, well stocked for a winter storm, and ready to tend to any wounds (physical or financial). You can handle a heat wave or a home invasion with equal poise. And when disaster hits, you know you can focus on what matters. By taking the small steps in this book, you've set yourself up for success no matter what comes your way. You're ready for anything!

TO DO

○ Take a deep breath

○ Take things one step at a time

○ Refer back to this book whenever you need to!